LOOKING BACK AT
MARITIME WIRRAL

Pat O'Brien

Willow
PUBLISHING

Willow Publishing

Willow Cottage, 36 Moss Lane,
Timperley, Altrincham,
Cheshire, WA15 6SZ

© Pat O'Brien 1989

ISBN 0 946361 27 4

Printed by The Commercial
Centre Ltd., Clowes Street,
Hollinwood, Oldham.

Also by the same author—'LOOKING BACK AT
ELLESMERE PORT'.

*This book is dedicated to my wife Norah Rowena,
who made it all possible.*

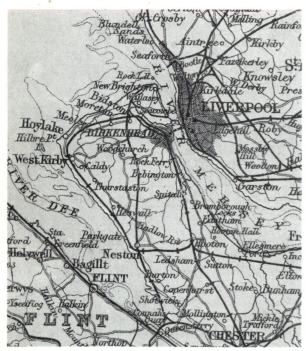

Cover photograph:
Eastham Ferry.

Title page:
**Constructing the Manchester Ship Canal at Ince in the
1890's.**

On the left was the old village school. The archway carried the main drive to Ince Hall, passing a sheet of water called 'The Old Rush Pit'.

Introduction

Although just outside Wirral, I include Ince in this maritime survey, because nearly forty years ago, the events of the past were vividly brought to life by the late Mrs Laura Proffit with whom I lodged. By the fireside in the old Abbot's House my interest in local history was born. Whilst the pictorial side deals mainly with the land bordering the sea, the text is a series of historical studies based on the adjoining coastal waters.

For information and valuable help I wish to thank the following people: the late Mrs A Anderson of Bromborough, the late Mr W F Bushell, MA, Cantab, late Headmaster of Birkenhead School, Mrs Marion Seal, Mr Hargreave, Mr Knight, Mr. R. Hunt, Chief Librarian, Mr D Jones, and the staff of Ellesmere Port Reference Library, the staff of Wallasey Reference Library, the late Mr Les Slack, Mr C Derbyshire, Mr J Fairclough of Ince. For help with information on 610 (County of Chester) Squadron. For the loan of pictures, I wish to thank the following people: Miss E Willshaw, Mr G Fisher, Mr D Darroch, Mr H O Williams and Mr J Dibble. To Mrs Beryl Newns, a deep sense of gratitude for typing my notes of ten years' research. To anyone whom I have inadvertently not mentioned, my sincere apologies.

PAT O'BRIEN 1989

Ince Lighthouse

The first lighthouse at Ince was built in 1838. By the end of 1877 the route along the south shore had become impassable, and on Christmas Eve the oil lamp in the lighthouse at Ince was extinguished. It was to be another six years before the lamp in Ince lighthouse was relit, when the meandering channel had once more moved across to the Cheshire shore. Lighthouses and lightships were inspected every month, and in the Summer of 1864, Ince lighthouse report shows a rapid deterioration of both the building and the lamps. In June 1865 the old lighthouse was demolished and a new one was built. This lighthouse was later demolished to make way for the Manchester Ship Canal.

The Mersey Estuary Channels in the 1870's

The Mersey Estuary has always been a hazard to shipping; charts were constantly being revised because of shifting sands. The great migration of the river's channels continued throughout the 1870's, and by 1876 the south channel past Stanlow and Ellesmere Port was fast closing up. The following year it was no longer navigable and the lightship Rival was removed from her station off Stanlow. In 1867 the river's currents exposed dangerous rocks near the navigable channel at Stanlow. The flat Lyon was equipped as a lighthouse and towed to a station off Stanlow.

The lighthouse at Stanlow was erected on an iron barge which was blocked up high and dry on the shore, in the charge of a Capt Evans. Later when the lightship became obsolete, he retired to a cottage on the Mersey side of Manisty's Mount. This was a hill created out of surplus soil excavated during the building of the Manchester Ship Canal. It covered a dangerous shoal of rocks called Pool Rocks, which had caused some notable shipwrecks.

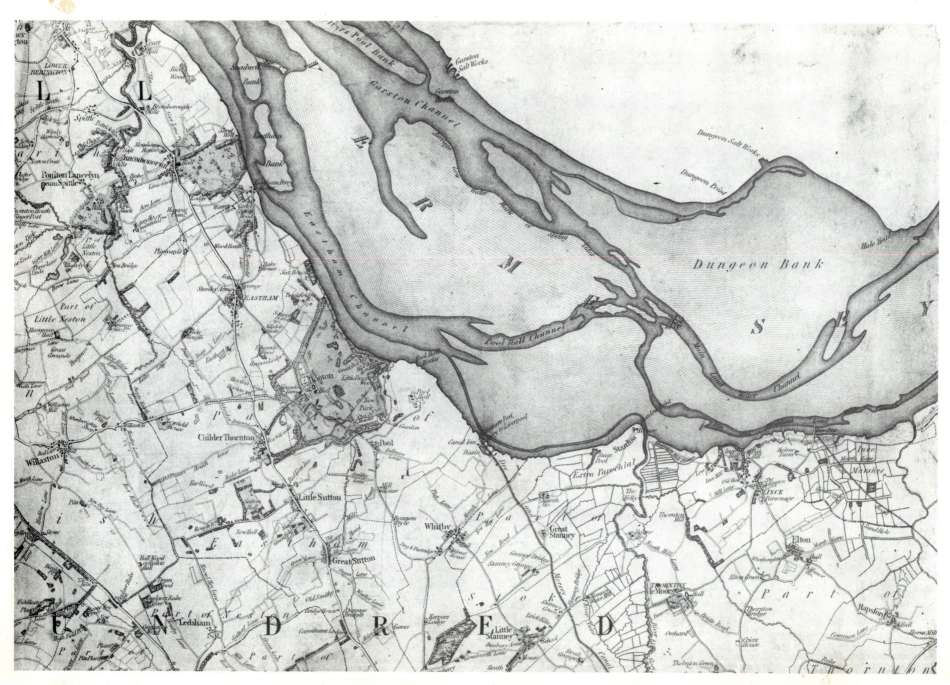

4

Wellington Square, the village centre.

A class at the village school.

Ince and Ince Hall

Ince has at times been called *Yny's* and *Ynes*, a Welsh word meaning an island. It is a sandstone island looking down on a coastline of marshland on either side. In the picture of New Row (overleaf), the large building at the top was the dining-hall of a 13th century Monastic Grange. Its unique fortified features are still to be seen. It had two Royal visits from Edward I in August 1277, and Edward II in October 1323. The road in the centre of New Row was known as Marsh Lane, and continued downhill past Rock Cottage to the Mersey shore where a ferry service operated to Liverpool from Ince Pier.

The Georgian manor house in the centre of Wellington Square was originally built as an inn for this ferry service. When the Manchester Ship Canal was being built the local squire Capt Park-Yates put up a stiff opposition, and all material for No. 2 Section had to be brought in by sea. When he died in the hunting field from the effects of a fall in 1896, his wife Clementina became Lady of the Manor and her word was law. No trains were allowed to run on Sundays, which were strictly to be observed as holy days for attending church. Before she died in 1935, Mrs Park-Yates shared out many of her household goods amongst her staff.

Ince in 1910, showing St James' Church. The second village school was built in 1869 and is now the village hall.

5

A local fête in the 1900's.

New Row, Ince.

Rock Cottage, Marsh Lane.

The Front Entrance, Ince Hall.

(*Left*): Ellesmere Port Lighthouse.
Before the 1890's Ellesmere Port lighthouse was of supreme importance to mariners on the Mersey estuary. To the North West was a very dangerous shoal of rocks called Pool Rocks after Pool Hall, the old Tudor Gothic house perched on the sandstone cliffs above. The main channel on the southern side of the Mersey Estuary was the Eastham Channel; opposite Pool Hall its main channel became much smaller and changed its name to the Pool Hall Channel. A branch of this wended its way through sandbanks to about 500 yards east of the lighthouse and then through a dredged channel to the Sea Lock beyond. A glance at the chart shows that this branch was scoured by the River Gowy whose outlet it was. Starting off as a canal terminal in 1795, it expanded and developed with both passenger and commercial traffic.

Ellesmere Port

Although the first Ordnance Map of 1841 shows the channel into Ellesmere Port coming along the Cheshire side from Pool Hall Deep and skirting a dangerous shoal of rocks called Pool Hall Rocks, because of shifting sandbanks a later chart of this area shows a diagonal channel coming across from the deep water channel on the Lancashire side to a point approximately 500 yds east of the Tidal Basin. This new channel was scoured clear by the River Gowy which followed the Cheshire bank to this spot, and then used it as an outlet. Several posts were erected on the western perimeter of this channel, and they are still in position today.

During the building of the Manchester Ship Canal a gap was left in the embankment built between Stanlow Point and Pool Hall opposite this channel. Because the Gowy was siphoned beneath the workings at Stanlow, the tide was allowed through this gap and into the Tidal Lock area, so that traffic to and from Ellesmere Port was not curtailed.

Because the tide for months had established a set route through the 250ft opening in the embankment, closing it was to prove no easy task.

On Saturday 11 July 1891, as soon as the Shropshire Union traffic had passed out and the tide was low, train loads of ballast were emptied as quickly as possible into the chasm from both sides. Slowly the heap rose above the level of the water, and people walked across what had been a deep gulf. At two o'clock on Sunday morning, to the dismay of everybody, the tide forced a small hole, which quickly became a large one, sweeping all the work away and taking repossession. Without delay a fresh start was made; this time thousands of tons of boulders were cast into the gap and heavy piles were driven in to prevent them moving about. Work went on all day Sunday, but to no avail. The sea washed away the huge boulders as if they had been marbles.

This second mishap prevented the usual packet (which had never missed since 1837), and its attendant tugs, getting to Ellesmere Port, and the penalty for stoppage was £300 per day. However, at the third attempt, with the aid of concrete and other material, the gap was finally sealed, and on the 16th the first flotilla of traffic from Ellesmere Port passed down the Ship Canal into the River Mersey.

A dredger keeping the gap open through the Manchester Ship Canal embankment.

Posts which still remain show the old channel from Ellesmere Port's Docks across the Mersey.

Eastham Pier.
Eastham Ferry Pier was built in 1872, for £6,000 and was held on a lease by Mr T W Thompson,

Ferry Hotel, Eastham. The boats on the ferry at this period were the 'Sylph' and 'Sprite'.

The Lease by Thomas, Abbot of the Monastery and Convent of St Werburg's, Chester, to Thomas Deane of Chester, barber, of a ferry boat in Pulpull, etc. No date but around the time of Henry VIII.

Eastham Ferry from the top of the Jubilee Arch.

Eastham Ferry.

Hooton Park Airfield

On the 22nd October 1917, No. 37 Wing, Royal Flying Corps, formed at The Oaks, Ledsham near Little Sutton, took under its control Nos. 90, 95 and 96 Squadrons and No. 4 Training Depot Station. No. 4 Training Depot Station was formed at Term Hill on 1st September 1917, but moved to Hooton Park on the 19th September 1917. This unit moved to Shotwick Airfield in 1919.

Hooton Hall and forty acres of Hooton Park were put up for sale, and this included the former airfield, by order of the Government Disposal Board on the 7th March 1922. In 1927 Liverpool's first Air Pageant was held at Hooton Park.

In 1928 a small band of enthusiasts decided to form The Liverpool & District Aero Club. At this time the landing ground was overgrown, and its hangars empty. However sufficient funds were collected to make a start, Sir Frederick Bowring and Sir Charles Nall-Cain each presented an aeroplane to start the Club, and on the 5th June 1928 active flying lessons began. By July 1931 the hangars were now in order, a small and attractive club house had been built, and the landing ground completely cleared.

To the right of the airfield the Polo Ground, situated in the middle of the Old Race Course, was made full use of by the Wirral Polo Club. The spare hangars were occupied by different companies assembling aircraft and aircraft engines.

In February 1936, a squadron of the Auxiliary Air Force was formed at Hooton Park. Its full title was No. 610 (County of Chester) Squadron of the Auxiliary Air Force. At this time only two of the squadron's officers had air experience, but six auxiliary officers and fifty-six airmen were enrolled. Formed as a Bomber Unit, it was originally equipped with Hart Bombers, and then

later with the Hawker Hind, a faster aircraft. In January 1938 it remustered as a fighter squadron. In October 1939 it moved to RAF Station, Wittering, Northants; in the Battle of Britain they operated from Biggin Hill. During August they had 40 enemy aircraft confirmed as being destroyed by them, for the loss of eight pilots.

The Squadron was reformed at Hooton Park in June 1946. At the same period the Wirral & District Aero & Gliding Club operated from here. At weekends they would instruct Liverpool Squadrons of the ATC. Sqn Ldr G C Wright, wartime Mosquito night intruder patrol pilot, and his staff, gave flying tuition in gliding and then in solo and dual flying.

In 1951, the Spitfires were replaced by Meteor MKIVF jet fighters. At the same time 611 West Lancashire Squadron, formerly based at Woodvale, moved to Hooton Park to make it their permanent station as well.

Mobile classrooms moved in, and the change-over from 400 mph spitfires to 650 mph jets was soon accomplished.

As well as the annual camp, the most important event of the year was 'Battle of Britain' week, held every September in Hooton Park. At this event in 1954 a tragic accident took place. A Meteor jet crashed into the trees just beyond the airfield during a demonstration by 610 Squadron of follow-my-leader flying. Though the show went on as if nothing had happened, a wisp of smoke rose all through the afternoon to remind those present that the squadron had lost one of its most experienced and well-liked pilots.

This was the third fatality 610 Squadron had suffered in twelve months.

Sadly all Auxiliary Air Squadrons were told early in 1957 that their services were no longer required. The airfield was put to other uses, and today the site is occupied by Vauxhall Motors.

H.O.C's inspection, 1938.

K 5476

1939

1949 inspection of Mark 22 Spitfires including two Horrords (Trainers).

Eastham Ferry, Landing Stages and Boats

The original licence for a ferry was at Poole and belonged to the Poole family. They had a grant for the ferry from the Black Prince on the 16th July, 1357. When it passed to the Abbey and Convent of St Werburg is not known. There is an undated Indenture of an Abbot Thomas of St Werburg [who was either Thomas Highfield (died 1527) or his successor Thomas Marshall (who was moved from there in 1529)] who leased one ferry boat at Eastham together with landing-stage and a cottage in a wood to Thomas Deane, barber, of Chester. After the Dissolution, the ferry passed from the Dean and Chapter of Chester to Sir Richard Cotton, and was sold by him. For a period the ferry was owned by the Stanley family. Near to the large sandstone blocks which is shown in an 1817 etching in Hanshall's *Cheshire*, there is a flight of steps to the shore; this is believed to be the site of the first ferry. Because the sandstone blocks appear in this etching they could be the second site. The third site shown is a slip running down close to the cliff, and a small dock for boats formed within its breakwater. On the outer slip is the paddle-steamer 'William Stanley'. The Stanley family had various boats named after them between 1820–40's. The fourth site can be seen in a picture which shows a large sandstone jetty with a horse and carriage, proceeding towards a ferry boat named 'Eastham Fairy' which was built in 1861. The iron pier, part of which still stands, was built in 1874.

In the 16th and 17th centuries there were many disputes between the different ferries. The principal ferry between Liverpool and the Cheshire side at a place called Birket Wood, was claimed by the King in 1626 and was known as 'King's Ferry'; he also laid claim to all other ferries. When King's Ferry was sold to private owners they claimed the same rights. The farmers of the

Entrance to Eastham Gardens.

Eastham boat on the Cheshire side, did usually pay the farmers of the King's Ferry for such 'fraught', or cargo and passengers they took in on the Liverpool side and carried to Cheshire. Rowing boats were first used, followed by single masted, and later by two-masted craft carrying jib and jigger sails. In July 1816 the steam-packet 'Princess Charlotte' commenced the Liverpool–Eastham service, and continued to sail twice daily each way.

Some of the early paddle steamers were: 'Lady Stanley' 1821, 'Maria' 1824; 'Lady Bulkeley' 1835; 'Royal Tar' 1836; 'Sprite' 1867. 'Athlete' 1890, was an iron twin-screw steamer.

A trio of paddle steamers: the 'Ruby', the 'Pearl', and the 'Sapphire' were the last to operate. The names of the ferries to which the various packets plied were painted on their paddle boxes, but each had a distinguishing symbol by which it could be recognised, for example, Eastham had a 'fox'. Later, funnels were painted with company colours; Eastham's had white and blue funnels. The ferry closed down in 1929.

Eastham Ferry

In the early days of steam, apart from stage-coach passengers, people mostly came here in the summer months to picnic and walk in Eastham Woods. When the hotel was built in 1845 by Sir W M Stanley the place became popular as a resort. Eighteen acres of gardens, pleasure grounds and zoological gardens were laid out. Famous artists gave displays, and there were also concert parties, pierrots and a band playing in the garden. At night there was dancing in the ballroom.

Blondin, the famous tightrope walker, visited here on several occasions. A Bromborough village boy shared the popularity of the great man by being wheeled in a barrow over the tightrope. He proved himself such a good subject that Blondin took him on tour for a number of years.

Eastham Gardens possessed at this time a far-famed menagerie. The unmistakable smell of lion was sniffed with rapture by children of the Victorian era; and the thrill of seeing the brown bear climb from its deep pit up the great wooden pole in the centre was one never to be forgotten.

A private local diary described August Bank Holiday in 1887:

'Eastham never had a better August Bank Holiday than Monday. The boats were filled and Mr I W Thompson, the spirited proprietor of the Ferry Hotel and Zoological Gardens, has cause to be satisfied with his catering for the public, for what with the Vol Besquetroupe and the marvellous little clown Baby Bumbo, the marionettes, wonderful pantomime by Messrs Chester and Lee, the two bands for the rotaries of the terpisdiors, the zoological collection and last and not least the site for the promised Ship Canal.'

The Jubilee Arch that stood at the entrance commemorating Queen Victoria's long reign, sadly disintegrated during the 1930's.

(Above left): **Fred Brook's Vauderville and Circus.**
(Left): **The Merry Madcaps, Eastham Garden.**

Sailing Clippers, Eastham Locks.

The Ship Canal at Eastham Locks.

The Powder Ships

The Corporation of Liverpool, to avoid the risk of an explosion at the docks, had made it compulsory for all ships coming into port to unload all the gunpowder which they had on board. This was conveyed in carts through the town to the Powder House on Brownlow Hill (near where Clarence Street now is), where it was stored until they were ready for sea again.

Becoming aware of the risk that was being incurred by carrying the powder in open carts back and forth through the town, in 1751 the Council purchased land in Liscard near the Black Rock which was then a sandy waste, and is now known as the Magazines. Before the enclosure of the commons early in 1800 all the lands north of Magazine Lane, on which the present New Brighton stands, was a waste of sandhills. Here sheds were erected and leased to various parties, to deposit their powder. In a number of privately owned, insecure slate-roofed buildings, in a small yard, 700 or 800 tons were commonly deposited, until 1852, when an Act of Parliament was passed and the powder was removed to the Hulks, near Eastham.

There were three 'Powder Ships' or Floating Magazines: 'The Swallow', 'The Mersey', and 'The Liverpool'. The 'Mersey' and the 'Liverpool' went out of service possibly before World War I. They were originally wooden warships over a hundred years old.

The 'Powder Ships' were painted yellow with wide red bands all round. In daytime they flew a red flag, 6ft by 3ft; at night time two lamps were hoisted on a central mast, one red the other white; the red one was six feet above the white one, both lights being about 3ft from the deck. A special oil was used in all lamps on board called 'Colzar', a vegetable oil. There was also a white light on the stern.

The 'Swallow' was overall wooden, 175ft long, the bottom being copper sheathed up to the water

The Powder Ship 'Swallow', offshore the Magazine Village, Eastham.

line; just above the water line it had hard wooden belting for fenders. On each side were five ports, with hinged door flaps, which would be pulled upright by hand to reveal a leather padded passage which was on an approximate level with the decks of the 'hoys' and used to roll the kegs of gunpowder in and out of the vessels.

On the foredeck was a storage cabin where ropes etc. were kept. At the stern end were the watchmen's quarters and the 'skipping' room. From the watchmen's quarters a companion ladder went down below to a platform which went right round the inside of the ship, with a wall of interlocked timber totally enclosing the magazines. Opposite the five ports in the outer hull on each side were five doors, with brass locks and hinges only opened by a master key. The doors were named after their position in the ship: the After Door, the After But One, Middle Port, Bow But One, and the Bow Door, each giving access to a stage 6ft square which was raised 3ft off the ship's bottom floor. During unloading a man would

stand on this stage, putting the barrels on a rail to ride inside where another man would catch them and stow them away. The interior magazine room was about 100ft long and 14ft high.

The 'skipping room' was where the damaged kegs were repaired. The floor was covered with leather, as was a capstan, where the kegs were placed to be repaired. The tools used were a copper hammer with a long head and a nail extractor, also toggles made of hard wood for replacing hoops on damaged kegs.

The 'truck' or top of the central mast had a lightning conductor, a copper spire fixed 3ft above it; the 'truck' itself was 80ft above deck. The copper conductor would go down the sheer legs which helped to support the central mast, under the ship and was fastened there. To test it, a man was hauled aloft in a bosun's chair to the top of the mast with a wire attached which he would place against the copper spire, the other end being affixed to a galvanometer on deck. When operating correctly it would ring bells on the meter.

Also on deck at the front end was a large bell used during fog or for emergency purposes. A large wooden tub was kept on either side, full of water in case of fire, with a supply of wooden buckets with rope handles. Also for fire protection there was a 'force' pump, operated with a wooden handle, the pump's supply of water coming from the river.

Inside the vessel the kegs were stored as near as possible to the outside water level, thus in case of collision the inside would be quickly flooded.

A large valve on deck operated an opening on the side of the ship, which would allow the sea in to flood the Magazine completely in half an hour. The ships were only allowed to hold 100 tons, though they had a capacity of 300 tons. The

Gunpowder known as the 'black powder' was kept in kegs, ranging from 5lbs to 100lbs.

The safety clothing and footwear for the watchmen consisted of large leather overboots with thick leather soles, and a smock made of a thick linen material with no buttons. There was a small office on shore, where the watchman would report before going on duty, to hand in any matches. Here too the copper hand-lamp was lit and brought aboard to light the lamps for the hours of darkness. The lamps would be lit well before the official lighting-up time.

The shifts were: day shift, one man from 7.00 a.m. till 5.00 p.m.; night shift, two men from 5.00 p.m. till 7.00 a.m. The following morning, they would split the watches, one on watch whilst the

other slept. During fog short rings would be given on the bell, and pilots on other boats would give short blasts on their whistles for the watchman to ring his fog bell until their vessel was clear of the Powder Ship.

The boats used for transhipping the kegs of 'black powder' were called the 'hoys'. They were about 60ft long, and operated under sail. They were black vessels with a red diamond on each side of the bow and a 6in red band right round the ship. They were constructed to withstand any weather. There were 4 hoys altogether.

Total Tonnage	Allowance	Name
	10	Eastham
	10	Birkenhead
50	25	Bebington
	25	Bromborough

The loading point was outside Garston Dock wall. The distance to the Powder Ship was approximately 3 miles and it took the hoys about 3 hours to reach it in bad weather, 1½ hours in normal.

The cargo was discharged as rapidly as possible on to the Magazine ship to catch mooring on the shore, otherwise they had to go back at night for 1/- to moor them on the evening tide. They were allowed to be moored on the foreshore opposite the Magazine, or Powder Ship.

When loading ships for overseas, the ships were only allowed to be charged by the hour at two points, in the Crosby Channel outside the Mersey Estuary, or in rough weather at a point off New Ferry, south of the pier. The area in the Crosby Channel was known as the Powder Ground. All fires had to be doused on cargo ships.

Rowing boats were stationed at all stages of the tide on shore, to enable a quick passage to the Magazine. Government Inspectors would visit the ships at infrequent intervals. At one time local quarries used to send handcarts down the track to the foreshore to collect explosives for quarrying.

(Left): **The Powder Ship 'Swallow', with a 'hoy' in the foreground.**

15

The Great Eastern

The Great Eastern was built on the Thames in 1858–60 to the plans of Brunel, the great engineer. Originally named Leviathan, she was the first of the big Atlantic liners and was driven by paddles, screws and sails. From the start she was an 'unlucky ship'—she stuck on the launchingways and was there for several months before she reached the water; her running costs were so high her 112 furnaces simply 'ate coal'. For a time she was chartered as a cable-layer. Then a Liverpool firm bought her as a floating advertisement and fun-fair during the Liverpool Exhibition of 1887. Anchored in the Mersey, she was visited by

thousands of people only too willing to wander over the largest vessel in the world. At last the old ship that had cost £732,000 to build was sold for £16,500 to the ship-breakers: they made a good bargain, for the material alone realized £58,000. She was broken up on Tranmere beach and many relics of her—chairs, mirrors, fittings and panelling—are still to be found scattered about Merseyside. The commemorative token illustrated here was probably sold on board the ship during the Liverpool Exhibition. There are more relics to be seen in the Great Eastern Hotel in New Ferry.

Her final break-up left a mystery that has never been solved, for the skeleton of an unknown man was found between the inner and outer hulls.

Commemorative token of the Great Eastern.

Port Sunlight Works in 1897

Soap Boiling Rooms: These were much too vast to be correctly called rooms—they were rather wide and lofty galleries. Their size can be gauged from the fact that they contained 84 pans, each holding 60 tons of liquid soap. Because vegetable oil was used, there was no unpleasant smell.

After the materials were boiled, they were passed to another room below for cooling. This was done in 'frames', great open-topped iron boxes into which the soap was poured. Once the soap was cold, the sides of the frames were opened and the massive, smooth blocks of soap were cut by machinery into slabs. These in turn were cut into bars, stamped and wrapped.

Cutting Soap, Port Sunlight.

Soap Boiling, Port Sunlight.

Lux Packing Room, Port Sunlight.

Lux Packing Room, Port Sunlight.

Port Sunlight.

The Lock, Port Sunlight.

The Quarantine Station

The quarantine station for Liverpool in the early years of the 18th century was the Sloyne, on the Cheshire side of the Mersey. Vessels were compelled to anchor there and were watched by a guard on the shore. Frequent escapes led to the assignment of an Admiralty sloop to watch suspected vessels and in 1721 the quarantine station was removed to Hyle Lake. Here the goods were aired on board flats or lighters, at the cost of the merchants themselves, and when they objected, at the expense of the Crown. The cost involved was enormous and many attempts were made by the customs officers to reduce it. They tried to secure the only available island—Hilbre, at the mouth of the Dee—for land lazarettos, but they were opposed by local landowners. Eventually, a floating lazaretto was anchored in Hyle Lake, but it proved inadequate for the increasing number of vessels entering port. Because this anchorage began to silt up, a new site was selected at New Ferry.

A dilemma occurred in 1886 that was to cause drastic changes. On May 2nd, a ship left the Mersey with 925 emigrants on board. By the time it reached Queenstown two had died on board from cholera, so it was refused admission, and had to return to Liverpool.

The 'Helvetia' was moored amidstream, and two ships the 'Var Cloud' and the 'Jessie Munn' were lashed to her, the former as a place for the healthy, the latter as a hospital ship. After some time warehouses were rented on shore and the healthy passengers brought there. Any persons showing symptoms of cholera were sent to the workhouse. There were twenty-four deaths on the Jessie Munn. This single incident led to the building of a Port Sanitary Isolation Hospital at New Ferry in 1875.

H.M. Training Ships on the Mersey.

Training Ship 'Conway', River Mersey.

TO EMIGRANTS.

CHOLERA.

CHOLERA having made its appearance on board several Passenger Ships proceeding from the United Kingdom to the United States of America, and having, in some instances, been very fatal, Her Majesty's Colonial Land and Emigration Commissioners feel it their duty to recommend to the Parents of Families in which there are many young children, and to all persons in weak health who may be contemplating Emigration, to postpone their departure until a milder season. There can be no doubt that the sea sickness consequent on the rough weather which Ships must encounter at this season, joined to the cold and damp of a sea voyage, will render persons who are not strong more susceptible to the attacks of this disease.

To those who may Emigrate at this season the Commissioners strongly recommend that they should provide themselves with as much warm clothing as they can, and especially with flannel, to be worn next the Skin; that they should have both their clothes and their persons quite clean before embarking, and should be careful to keep them so during the voyage,—and that they should provide themselves with as much solid and wholesome food as they can procure, in addition to the Ship's allowance to be used on the voyage. It would, of course, be desirable, if they can arrange it, that they should not go in a Ship that is much crowded, or that is not provided with a Medical Man.

By Order of the Board,

S. WALCOTT,
SECRETARY.

Colonial Land and Emigration Office,
8, Park Street, Westminster,
November, 1853.

Training Ship 'Conway', Rock Ferry.

By the Pier, New Ferry.

The 'Indefatigable', Training Ship.

20

The Navy Press-Gang

In the year 1353, during the reign of Edward III, the State assumed the power of impressment for the purpose of replenishing the Navy, forcing men to join whether they were willing or not.

Ships of the Royal Navy would visit ports to obtain crews, or a permanent guardship would be based in a port, and used both as a depot and a means of boarding incoming ships.

In the Mersey the 'Princess', was a permanent guardship for pressed men and volunteers, lying in the river opposite Georges Dock. The press-gang selected from among the most fierce and unscrupulous sailors. Their favourite shore haunts, the inns in Pool Lane or South Castle Street, were dangerous, not only because of the presence of the press-gang, but because their hostessess, willing to hide men while their money lasted, were often ready to sell them when their purses were empty. Often the sailors of incoming vessels would leap into the river as they entered the Mersey and swim to the Cheshire shores to avoid detection.

In 1759 HMS Vengeance arrived short-handed in the Mersey, and lay in wait. Presently there entered the river a whaling ship just home from the long Greenland voyage. The cutters of the Vengeance boarded her and the crew of the whaler was ordered to go on board the warship. They refused and a fierce battle took place. The whalers with long blubber knives and harpoons drove the man-of-war's men back to their cutters and sailed on. The battle continued on land, where all but six managed to escape.

One industrious mechanic was pressed whilst at work and was forthwith sent off. His wife, left penniless with a child to support, was brought to starvation point, and in her distressed state was tempted to purloin a trifling article from a shop in order to procure food. At that time robbery from a shop, however small, was a capital offence; she was detected, convicted and executed, and her infant, whilst being fed from her breast, was torn from her arms at the foot of the gallows.

The Pier, Rock Ferry.

The Pier, Rock Ferry.

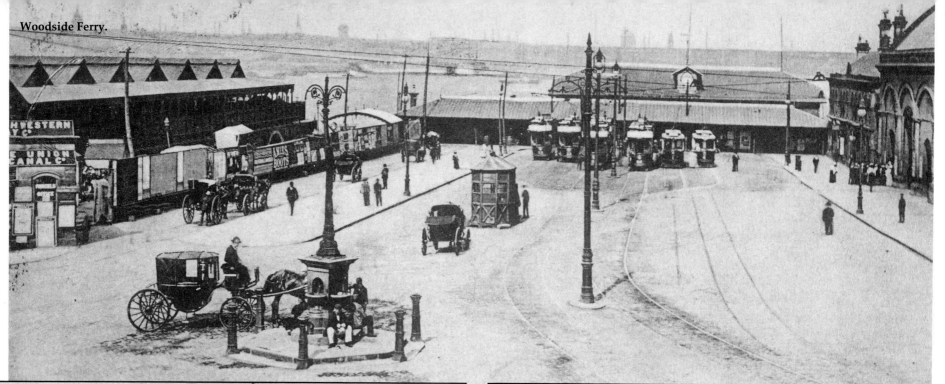

Woodside Ferry.

oodside Ferry.

Birkenhead Dock Disaster, March 1909.

'The Lusitania' in the Mersey.

...ce on the Mersey.

Accident, Seacombe Landing Stage, February 1909.

Egremont Ferry, after 1908.

Egremont Ferry, c.1908.

The Mersey Submarine Miners

In 1838 a Col. Pasley of the Royal Engineers successfully experimented to remove the wrecks of ships that were endangering shipping lanes at busy southern ports. Gunpowder was sealed in a leaden cylinder to keep it waterproof, and enclosed in a wooden buoy, which was linked by a waterproof cable to a Daniells battery of ten cells, the ignition system. Thus the sea-mine was born.

In 1886 Major-General Sir A Clarke, whilst Inspector General of Fortifications, stated that four Companies of Volunteer Submarine Miners had been formed for the defence of the Clyde, Tyne, Mersey and Severn.

The Mersey Division Royal Engineers Submarine Miners' headquarters were on board 'HMS Annettin' in the Kings Dock, Liverpool. Their duties included the laying of mines in the Mersey which were suspended at varying heights from the bed of the estuary and secured by chains. These were controlled from the Perch Rock Battery. The laying of ground mines was controlled from the Liverpool side and the working of searchlights in the Mersey defences.

Many of the men were from Wallasey, a large number being employees of the Wallasey Ferries Department. Their annual fifteen-day camps were held at New Brighton on land known as the Warren. Using the fort as their operational headquarters the miners would go into the river each day to practise mine laying. A member, the late Mr A Joynson who joined in 1897, stated that the captain in charge of his particular company then, was Dr J W Lloyd of Hoylake, father of the late Rt Hon Selwyn Lloyd, a former Speaker of the House of Commons.

In 1908 the name was changed to 'The Mersey Division RE Electrical Engineers'. In 1909 it was called 'The Lancashire Fortress Engineers', both based on HMS Annettin in Clarence Dock.

The Mersey Division Royal Engineer's (Volunteers) Submarine Miners, 1897.

The Fort, New Brighton.

(Top left): Testimonial to Lieut Col Knight, Commanding Officer of The Mersey Div RE Vol Submarine Miners.

(Top right): Officers of the 'Submarine Miners'.

(Below): The Magazines Promenade.

Shipwrecks in the Dee Estuary

The quiet shorelines of Wirral have been witness to many scenes of tragedy and destruction, in the aftermath of storms. Here are eye-witness accounts of some tragic shipwrecks that occurred on our shores.

'In a hurricane-force storm on Thursday 19th, 1775, the Parkgate packet brig 'Nonpareil', with Samuel Davis, master, foundered on Hoyle Bank and was destroyed. This wind continued for nearly thirty hours. The 'Nonpareil' had aboard a large number of passengers and a rich cargo of spices, silks, jewels and other things roughly to the value of £20,000. Bodies cast upon the sands below Talacre and Gronant on the Flintshire shore were robbed and nineteen beach ghouls were apprehended', said the Chronicle of November 13, 1775.

In the succeeding week's newspaper the Chester Port Authorities advised jewellers, goldsmiths, and particularly travelling chapmen, to be cautious in purchasing any part of the rich cargoes which, they had reason to believe, had been taken from the wrecks and detained or concealed.

Another terrible tragedy was that of the Dublin packet, the 'Earl of Moira', lost near Leasowe in August, 1821. She was laden with passengers, and the last struggles of many who perished were most distressing, but the callous heartlessness of the Wallasey people is a scandalous record. The Hoylake life-boat went out and nobly rescued many, but the Wallasey boats merely went out for plunder, and as the huge waves carried off the trunks or property of the unfortunate passengers, they were seized by those in the boats, while the men refused to catch the cork fender with rope attached which was thrown to them from the ship.

A poor young mother clasped her two children, aged two years and eight months; the waves dashed against her and buried the children

New Brighton sands.

for a minute. When the water receded the children were dead, and a few moments later the same fate overtook the mother. Two soldiers had a deserter in charge. They dutifully remained by him until he was washed overboard and drowned. One of the soldiers was then carried under the boom, where he clung to one of the stays. As the vessel lifted he was several times above water, but at last, calling piteously for mercy, he succumbed. The men, women and children in the forepart of the ship were the most exposed to the furious tempest, and those who had taken to the rigging witnessed the most appalling death scenes, but the wreckers cared for nothing but stripping and plundering the bodies cast up by the tide. It is sad to state that the captain, mate and crew were all intoxicated. The steward and one or two others did their best but many lives were lost.

On the 7th January, 1839, three emigrant ships, the 'St Andrew', the 'Lockwoods', and the 'Pennsylvania', had almost reached Holyhead, after leaving Liverpool the previous day, when the wind changed to the north-west and became a hurricane. They at once put back for the Mersey, but the wind was so strong that it smashed the vessels to pieces on the Burbo and West Hoyle Banks. The Liverpool lifeboat, towed by the tug 'Victoria' managed to reach the scene and saved many lives. A great many however were drowned and washed ashore on the nearby coast.

New Brighton Pier.

New Brighton

The first pier or jetty was built of wood, with a small run-out stage on lines, used at low tide, which was hauled up on the flood tide by means of a windlass worked by a horse treading in a circular track. On the ebbtide, each departing steamer pulled the stage out to enable the next steamer to land.

There was a long flight of steps leading from the pier to the shore, up and down which collectors carried a small pay box to enable the collection of tolls on the pier at high water, or on the beach at low water where the passengers disembarked via the run-out stage.

A new pier was opened in 1867. The ferry suffered two mishaps, first during its reconstruction in 1928 when damage was caused by the steamer SS 'Galilio' crashing through it, and in 1907 during a heavy gale when the stage became detached from its moorings and floated well out to sea.

Lifeboat at New Brighton.

Wreck of the Landing Stage, March 17th, 1907.

Leasowe and Meols

The Leasowe embankment, protecting part of the Great Meols shore, was constructed under an Act passed in 1829. Leasowe Castle is reputed to have been built in 1593, by the fifth Earl of Derby. In 1802 it was purchased by a Mrs Booth, and during her occupancy it was frequently turned into a receiving house and hospital for the survivors of shipwrecks.

At Meols, in 1891 the spring tides dislodged some drift-sand, revealing the foundations of ancient British huts, which had been made of wattle-work coated with clay, and arranged so as to form an irregular village street.

The spaces between the houses were marked with the hoofs of horses shod with round shoes and with the foot-marks of cattle, pigs and sheep. There were also the very clear marks of cart-wheels and human footprints, all of which had been filled in by light-blown sands, and thus preserved.

Submerged forest, Meols.

Leasowe Lighthouse.

Leasowe embankment, camp and Lighthouse.

Moreton Village, Birkenhead.

Moreton

Though referred to as Moreton, its full title is the township of Moreton-cum-Lingham, which literally means 'long Marsh'.

In 1801 the population was 210, and in 1846 there were 330. At this time there were 88 dwelling houses, three licensed: 'The Plough Inn and Druids' Arms', 'The Farmer's Arms', and 'The Coach and Horses'.

In the Parish church, Christ Church, is a memorial to William Inman of the famous Inman Shipping Line, and carved on it is a line which says, *'The Originator of Steamship Emigration'*.

Between 1829–50 the embankment mentioned at Leasowe was extended, by Liverpool Corporation, to link up with the promenade at Hoylake. This work was initiated in order to prevent the low-lying lands of Meols and Moreton from being flooded by the sea in consequence of the continual erosion of the sand dunes.

The Embankment, Moreton.

The Smithy, Moreton.

Hoylake

This was the name of a roadstead, now silted up, off the north-west coast of Wirral, east of Hilbre, inside the Hoyle Bank. On the 12th June, 1690, William III went from here to Carrickfergus, to command against Londonderry. The point from which he embarked is still known as King's Gap.

In Little Meols were erected two of the first lighthouses in England under authority of the Act of 1761, by the Corporation of Liverpool. In 1766 they were described as *'the brick lighthouse at Highlake, and the low wooden lighthouse'*. The wooden one stood on the spot still occupied by the lower lighthouse, which was built in 1865 to replace an intermediate small brick one. The upper brick lighthouse was a structure similar to that still remaining at Leasowe, 70 feet tall, and was rebuilt in 1865. Coal fires were at first used for illumination, but in 1772 Mr Holden's invention for reflecting lights was adopted for all lighthouses of the port of Liverpool.

Launching the Lifeboat.

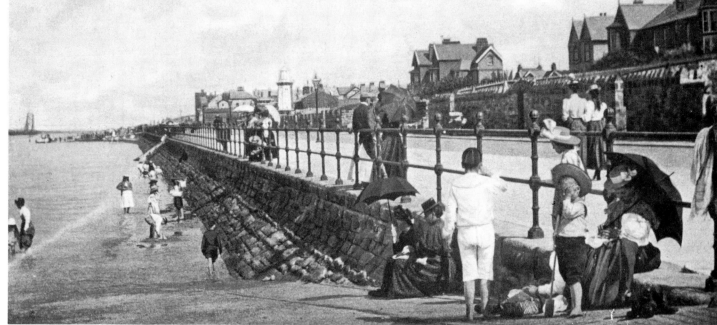

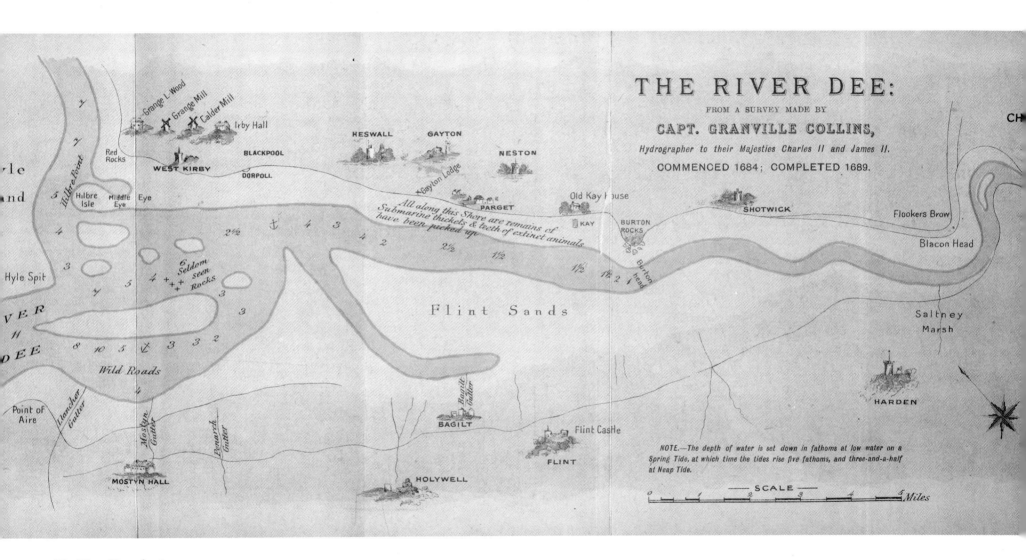

THE RIVER DEE:

FROM A SURVEY MADE BY

CAPT. GRANVILLE COLLINS,

Hydrographer to their Majesties Charles II and James II.

COMMENCED 1684; COMPLETED 1689.

CH

Grange L. Wood
Grange Mill
Calder Mill
Irby Hall

Red Rocks

BLACKPOOL

WEST KIRBY

DORPOLL

HESWALL

GAYTON

NESTON

Hilbre Point

Hilbre Isle
Middle Eye
Eye

Gayton Lodge

Old Kay House

SHOTWICK

Flookers Brow

PARGET

KAY

BURTON ROCKS

Blacon Head

All along this Shore are remains of Submarine thickets & teeth of extinct animals have been picked up

Burton head

Hyle Spit

6 Seldom seen Rocks

Flint Sands

Saltney Marsh

VER

DEE

Wild Roads

HARDEN

Point of Aire

Llanchers Gutter

Mostyn Gutter

Penarth Gutter

Bagilt Gutter

BAGILT

Flint Castle

FLINT

NOTE.—The depth of water is set down in fathoms at low water on a Spring Tide, at which time the tides rise five fathoms, and three-and-a-half at Neap Tide.

MOSTYN HALL

HOLYWELL

SCALE

0   1   2   3   4   5 Miles

The River Dee, chart.

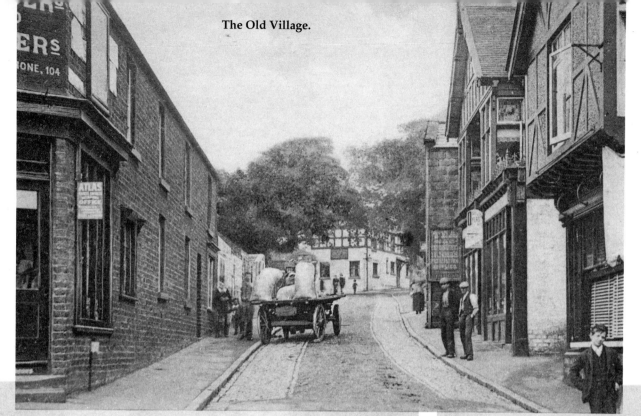

The Old Village.

West Kirby

The name literally means *'Village with a church'*. 'West' distinguishes it from the other Kirby in Wallasey.

The dedication of the parish church to St Bridget raises speculation as to whether it was due to British influence, or Norse incursions. After the Norsemen were defeated at the Battle of Clontarf, Dublin, the Anglo-Saxons permitted them to settle in various places in Wirral and Chester.

The loss of life on the coast used to be very great, and an open bier was kept at West Kirby, for carrying the bodies of those found drowned on the shore. Those unknown to the parish were buried on the north side of the churchyard. It was the recognized duty of anyone who found a body on the shore to bring it in for burial. If instead of doing so he should 'leave it to the mercy of the winds and waves' he would be considered to have disregarded the sacred rights of the dead.

The Lakeside.

Hilbre Island

Hilbre

Originally this was called *'Hildeburgs island'* named after an Anglo-Saxon holy woman, for there was a church on Hilbre from early times. In 1139 the Abbey of St. Werburgs, Chester, bought the village of West Kirby, which included the islands of Hilbre, for an annual payment of 30 shillings, from the Abbey of St Evroult in Normandy. They established a cell of two monks here. Between 1232 and 1237, John the Scot, Earl of Chester, gave the cell ten shillings a year for the light of St Mary. Presumably this light, hung in the chapel, acted as a beacon to ships entering and leaving the Dee estuary. After the Dissolution it passed through various hands, and did not return to the Dean and Chapter until the Restoration of the monarchy. In 1813 it had a public house for its only habitation. Trinity House and the Liverpool Dock Board had a station there for the supervision of the buoyage of the Dee and Conway Bay; this station discontinued in 1876. The Dock Board erected their station in 1841 as a look-out in connection with the telegraph services maintained at Bidston Lighthouse; and when the semaphore system was disused, after 1858, Hilbre was connected by telegraph with stations on the line from Liverpool to Holyhead.

The Lifeboat House, Hilbre Island.

Hilbre Island.

Caldy

In 1086 this was part of the Manor of Calders; this is an old English word which means *'cold arse'*, a hill name. It alluded to the prominent hill on which lie Grange and Caldy. It gave its name also to the 'Hundred of Caldy', within the Hundred of Wirral. A hundred within a hundred does not seem to be known elsewhere. Is it because all the manors named as part of it belonged to Robert of Rhuddlan who held the title of Earl of Chester, or the partial survival of the semi-independent Norse colony permitted to settle here.

Calday Grange School was founded in 1636 by William Clegg, of Caldy Grange. At the end of the 18th century the family had financial difficulties and the then Mr William Clegg was confined to Chester Castle for debt. Some time later when found to be seriously ill, he was sent home to die. His eldest son was so affected by it all that he left home, taking with him a piece of his ancestral soil, vowing he would never return until he could redeem the property. But, alas for his good resolves, he died in America, and in his trunk with his clothes was found the treasured remnant of the old estate.

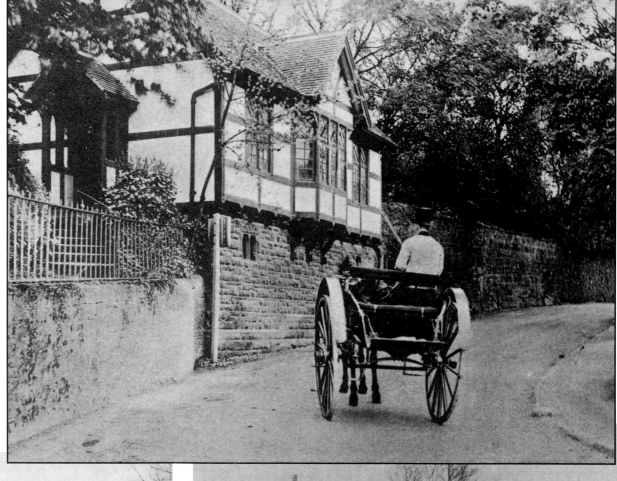

The Glen, Caldy.

Caldy Grange School and House.

Irby

Thurstaston

Irby Old Hall.

Thurstaston Shore.

Irby Village.

Cottages by Dawpool, Thurstaston.

Heswall

Parkgate

Dawstone Road, Heswall.

Bird's-eye view of Parkgate and Heswall.

Mostyn House School, (The Beagle Kennels).

The Village, Heswall.

Parkgate.

Burton

(Above): The Quakers' graves inscriptions are now completely obliterated. They were the last resting place of a man and wife, who were very early members of the Society of Friends. In 1890 part of the inscription could be read, 'The Body of Ell----1663', Quaker of Ellthorns or Hellthorns, a farm near Denhall Lane. Nearby is 'Friendshall' which tradition describes as the meeting house of the Quakers.

Shotwick

Shotwick was once a very important place. Since mediaeval times it was a ford into North Wales. For nearly a hundred years it took the place of Chester as a port. Throughout the 18th Century the ford was in continual use, the last recorded crossing being in 1796. The present approach leads from the old Chester– Parkgate turnpike road which was opened in 1789.

In the south-west wall of the churchyard can be seen an iron ring, said to have come from the quay where it was used for mooring.

Woodbank Toll Gate.

(Above): **Shotwick Village.**   *(Below):* **Shotwick Church.**